Dwell
In
Dreams
Dance
In
Daylight

LOVE
IS
OUR
RELIGION

Galactic
Grace
Grounded
Goals

Twilight
Tales
And
Moonlit
Musings

Vibes
Of
Love
And
Unity

Dive
Into
Dreams
Swim
In
Stars

Woven
With
Wonder
Kissed
By
Stars

HIPPIE
HEARTS
BLOOM

Life's
A
Trip
Enjoy

Sun's
Warmth
Moon's
Serenity

Soulful
Sojourns
Mystic
Musings

Room
With
A
Dream

WOVEN
WITH
WHIMSY
TIED
TO
TRUTH

Soul
Stitched
With
Starlight

Seek
Solace
in
Starlight

NATURE'S
RHYTHM
HEART'S
RHYME

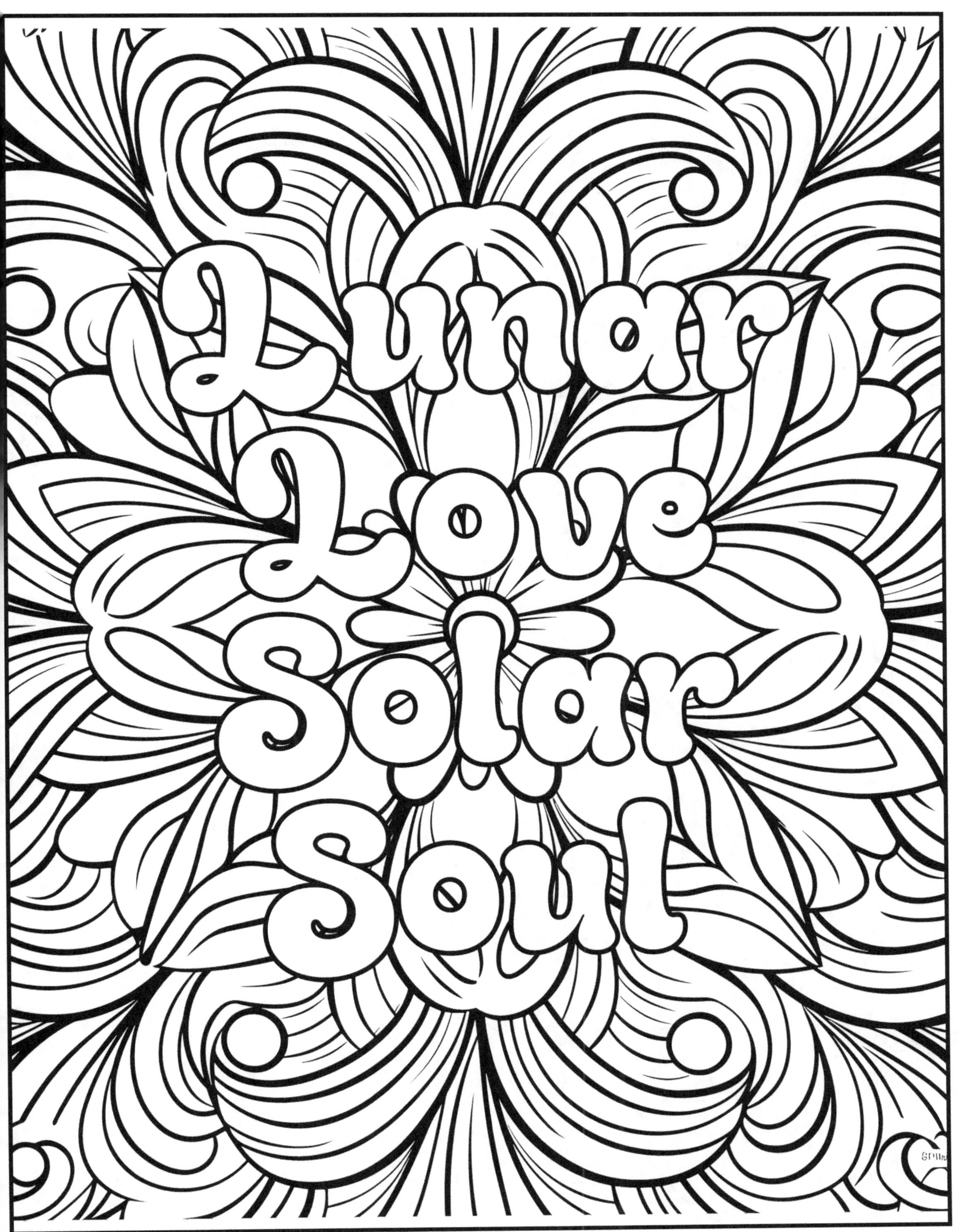
Lunar
Love
Solar
Soul

Lost
Stars
Found
Dreams

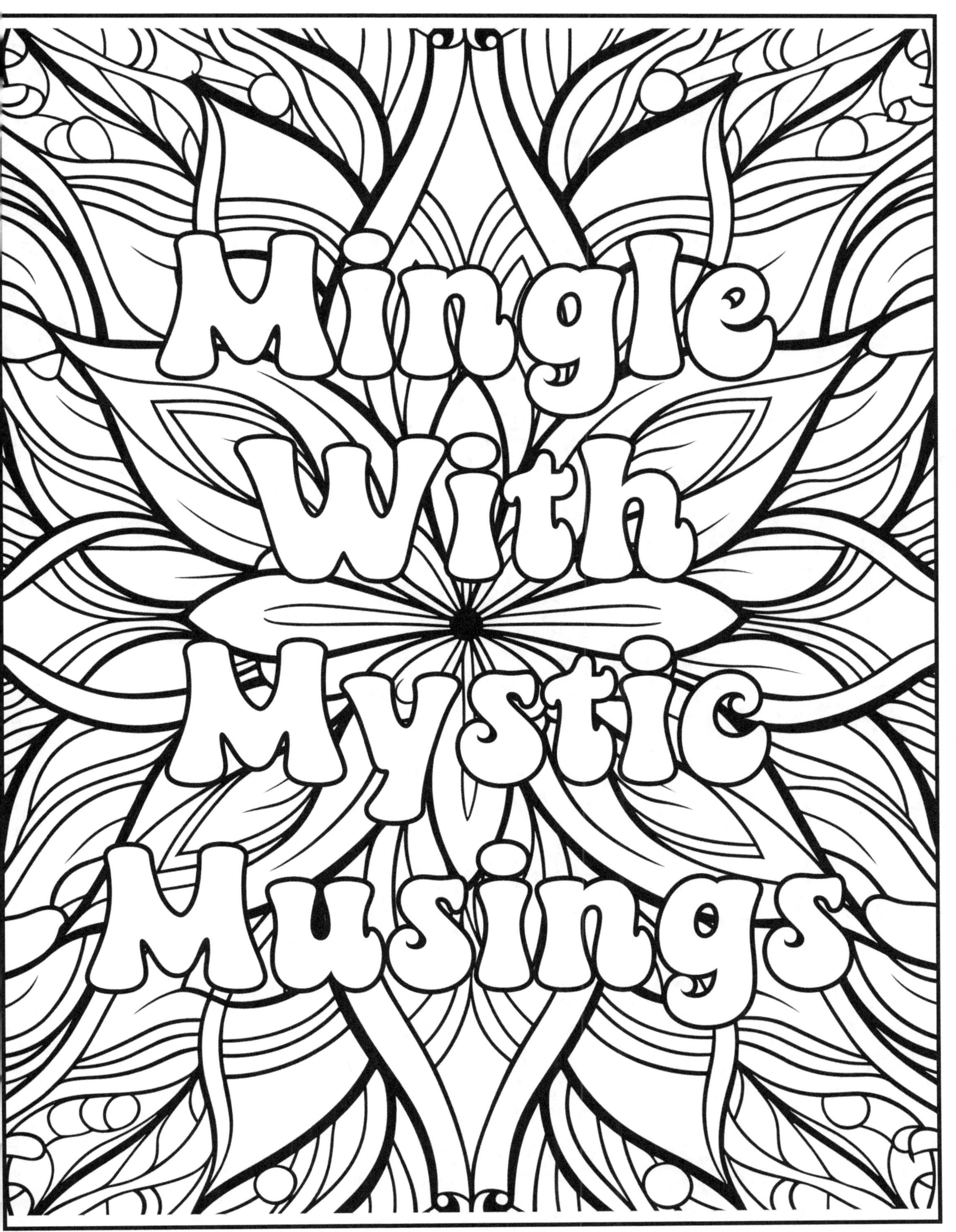

Mingle
With
Mystic
Musings

Let
Your
Soul
Sing

Living
Free
Loving
Wild

Cherish
Every
Sunrise

FREE
YOUR
MIND
SOUL

In
Every
Echo
Eternity

Fear
Less
Love
More

Chase
Sunsets
Not
Troubles

Journey
Through
Joyous
Junctures

Lost
In
Love's
Labyrinth

Life's
Art
Peace
Signs

Make
Tea
Not
War

Hippie
Soul
Gypsy
Heart

Dive
Deep
Dream
Different

SOULFUL
STROLLS
STARRY
SIGHTS

Groove
With
The
Galaxy

Earth
Child
Star
Born

TRUST
THE
JOURNEY

Flower
Child
Spirit

Crafted
From
Cosmos
And
Courage

Living
Wild
Loving
Kind

Love's
Endless
Echo

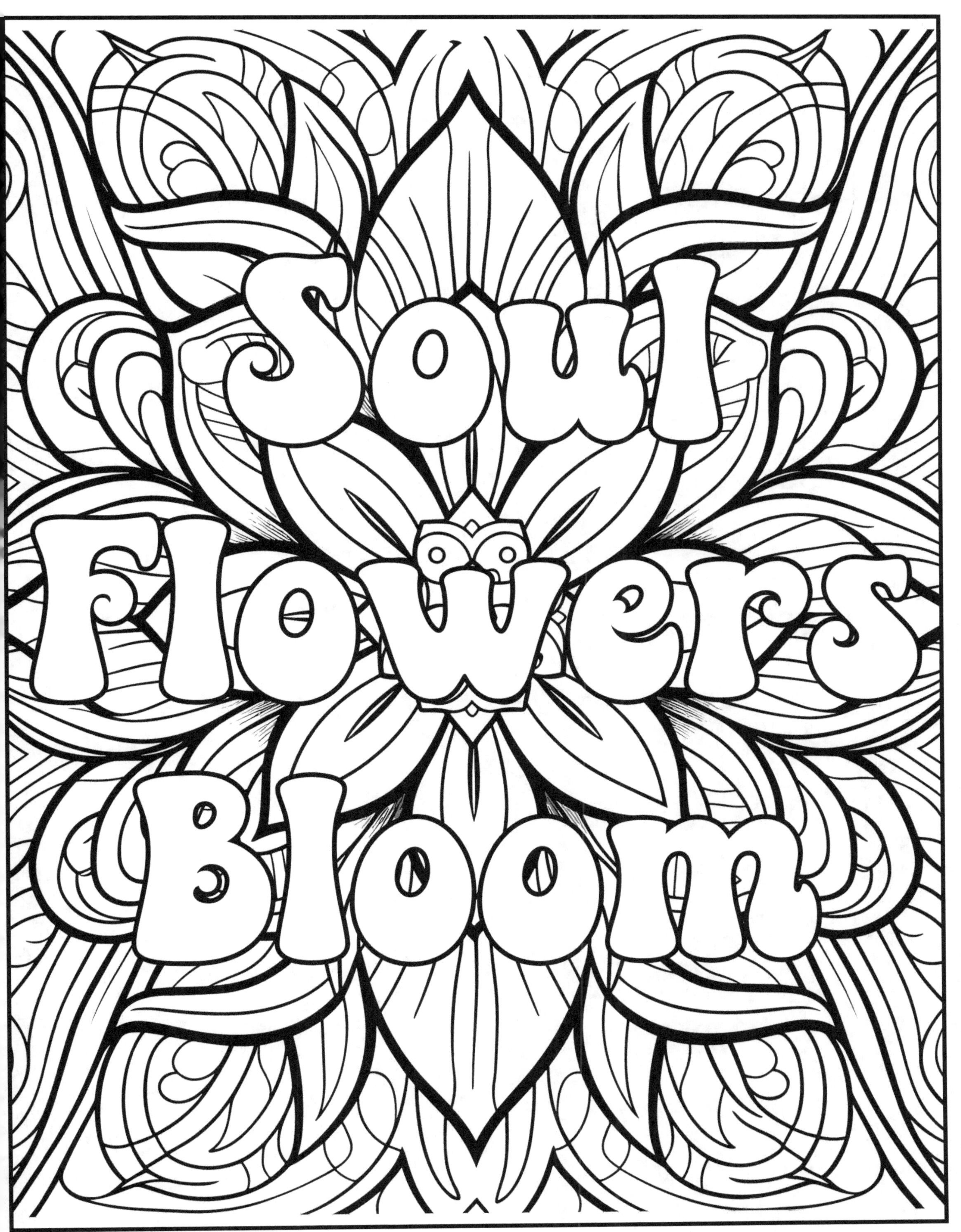

Soul
Flowers
Bloom

Stay
Wild
Moon
Child

Peace
Over
Power

Hippie
Heart
Open
Mind